ASIAN FAVORITES

Simple Dream
Simple Dream Publishing Inc.

Foreword

This eclectic collection of recipes takes you on a culinary trip of Asian delights. Besides such well-known recipes as Teriyaki Chicken, Pad Thai and spring rolls, you will discover the wonderful flavors of more exotic fare from this part of the world. Stir-fried Lemongrass Chicken from Vietnam, Beef in Tamarind from Indonesia and Fish with Green Mango Sauce from Thailand are just some examples of dishes that will entice you to prepare something out of the ordinary for family and guests. Looking for a special dessert? Why not try the Indonesian Coconut Pancakes. Asian cuisine is synonymous with healthy eating. Cooking techniques using a wok and steamer bring out the best in fresh ingredients such as fish and crispy vegetables and cut down on preparation time. The fabulous color pictures that accompany the recipes will inspire you to add some Asian flair to your cooking repertoire.

Abbreviations

tbsp = tablespoon

tsp = teaspoon

fl oz = fluid ounce

in = inch

lb = pound

g = gram

oz = ounce

°F = degree Fahrenheit

Method

Place shallots, chili peppers, lime leaves, ginger, and broth in a saucepan and bring to the boil over a high heat. Reduce heat and simmer for 3 minutes.

Add fish, shrimp, mussels, and mushrooms and cook for 3–5 minutes or until fish and seafood are cooked. Discard any mussels that do not open after 5 minutes cooking. Stir in lime juice and fish sauce. To serve, ladle soup into bowls, scatter with coriander (cilantro) leaves and accompany with lime wedges.

Note:

Straw mushrooms are one of the most popular mushrooms used in Asian cooking and are easy to find in cans. Oyster mushrooms are also known as abalone mushrooms and range in color from white to gray to pale pink. Their shape is similar to that of an oyster shell and they have a delicate flavor. Oyster mushrooms should not be eaten raw as some people are allergic to them in the uncooked state.

Ingredients

4 red or golden shallots, sliced

2 fresh green chili peppers, chopped

6 kaffir lime leaves

4 slices fresh ginger

8 cups fish, chicken or vegetable broth

8oz boneless firm fish fillets, cut into chunks

Hot-and-Sour Seafood Soup

12 medium raw shrimp, shelled and deveined

12 mussels, scrubbed and beards removed

1 cup oyster or straw mushrooms

3 tbsp lime juice

2 tbsp Thai fish sauce (nam pla)

fresh coriander (cilantro) leaves

lime wedges

Method

Peel the outer covering from the lemongrass stalk, then finely chop the lower white bulbous part and discard the fibrous top.

Place the broth, fish sauce, sugar, lemongrass, chili pepper, garlic, and ginger in a saucepan. Bring to the boil, then reduce the heat and simmer, covered, for 10 minutes to release their flavors.

Add the chicken slices to the broth and cook for 2 minutes, then add the carrot, celery, and green onions (scallions) and cook for a further 5 minutes or until the vegetables and chicken are cooked and tender. Add the lime juice and herbs to the broth and heat through. Garnish with the shredded green onion.

Thai Broth with Chicken and Vegetables

Ingredients

1 stalk lemongrass

5 cups chicken broth

4 tbsp Thai fish sauce

1 tbsp superfine (caster) sugar

1 red chili pepper, deseeded and sliced

1 clove garlic, sliced

1in piece fresh root ginger, thinly sliced

3 skinless boneless chicken breasts, thinly sliced

1 carrot, cut into matchsticks

1 stick celery, sliced

5 green onions (scallions), 4 sliced, 1 shredded, to garnish

1 lime, juice squeezed

1 tbsp each of roughly chopped fresh coriander (cilantro), mint, and basil

Method

Blanch cabbage leaves in boiling water and cut away any tough sections from the base.

Cut white ends from green onions (scallions) and finely chop four white heads. Slice two lengthwise for garnish. Slice green stalks into strips.

Mix chopped green onions (scallions) and 2 tbsp of the coriander with pork and shrimp. Season with pepper.

Into each cabbage leaf, place 1 tbsp of mixture. First fold the leaf base then outer edges over it, and roll up. Carefully tie up each roll with a length of green onion (scallion) then place the packages gently into boiling broth and cook for 6 minutes.

Lift parcels into bowls, pour a cup of broth over each and garnish with remaining sliced green onions (scallions) and coriander. Dip rolls into fish sauce when eating.

Ingredients

1 cup pork, minced

½ cup prawns, minced

6 green onions (scallions)

4 tbsp coriander, finely chopped

24 cabbage leaves

6¼ cups chicken or pork broth

2½ tbsp fish sauce

Cabbage Packages in Soup

Method

Heat oil in a wok over a medium heat. Add pork, water chestnuts, and lemongrass and stir-fry for 5 minutes or until pork is browned. Remove from wok and set aside to cool.

Place pork mixture, lime juice, and fish sauce in a bowl and mix to combine. Add beansprouts, green onions (scallions), mint, coriander (cilantro) and black pepper to taste, and toss gently.

Line a serving platter with lettuce leaves, then top with mangoes and pork mixture. Sprinkle with chopped hazelnuts or pecans.

Note:

This salad can be prepared to the end of step 2 several hours in advance. Cover and keep at room temperature. If preparing more than 2 hours in advance store in the refrigerator and remove 30 minutes before you are ready to assemble and serve it.

Minted Pork and Mango Salad

Ingredients

1 tbsp vegetable oil

2 cups lean ground pork

2 tbsp canned water chestnuts, chopped

2 stalks fresh lemongrass, finely chopped

or 1 tsp dried lemongrass, soaked in hot water

until soft

2 tbsp lime juice

1 tbsp fish sauce

4 tbsp bean sprouts

3 green onions (scallions), chopped

4 tbsp chopped fresh mint

2 tbsp chopped coriander (cilantro)

freshly ground black pepper

½ lb/8 oz assorted lettuce leaves

2 mangoes, peeled and sliced

2 oz toasted hazelnuts or pecans, chopped

Method

To make filling, heat peanut oil in a frying pan over a high heat, add shallots, ginger and chili pepper and stir-fry for 2 minutes. Add pork and stir-fry for 4–5 minutes or until pork is brown. Stir in coriander (cilantro) and kechap manis and cook for 2 minutes longer. Remove pan from heat and set aside to cool.

To assemble, place 2 tbsp of filling in the center of each wrapper, fold one corner over filling, then tuck in sides, roll up and seal with a few drops of water.

Heat vegetable oil in a wok or large saucepan until a cube of bread dropped in browns in 50 seconds. Cook the spring rolls, a few at a time, for 3–4 minutes or until crisp and golden. Drain on absorbent kitchen paper and serve with chili sauce for dipping.

Pork Spring Rolls

Ingredients

24 spring roll (wonton) wrappers, each
5 in square vegetable oil for deep-frying
sweet chili sauce (for dipping)

Pork and coriander filling

2 tsp peanut oil
3 red or golden shallots, chopped

2 tsp finely grated
fresh ginger
1 fresh red chili, seeded
and chopped
1 lb pork mince
2 tbsp chopped fresh coriander (cilantro) leaves
2 tbsp kechap manis

Method

Beat the eggs in a bowl, stir in beansprouts, green onions (scallions), and crabmeat, and add salt and pepper to taste.

Add oil to a frying pan to cover the base, heat it, and drop in all of the crab mixture, 1 heaping tbsp at a time.

Fry until golden-brown on one side, then turn and brown the other side.

Remove from pan, and keep warm.

To make the sauce, blend together the cornstarch and sugar in a pan, add soy sauce, chicken broth, and fish sauce.

Slowly bring to the boil over a low heat, stirring all the time. Cook for 3 minutes (or until sauce is thickened). Stir the sherry into the mixture before serving.

Ingredients

3 eggs

1 cup bean sprouts

3 green onions (scallions), chopped

1¾ cups crabmeat

salt and cracked black peppercorns

oil (for deep frying)

Crabmeat Fritters

Sauce

2 tsp cornstarch

1 tbsp sugar

3 tbsp soy sauce

1 cup chicken broth

1 tbsp fish sauce

2 tbsp dry sherry

Method

Remove head, fins, and tail from fish and cut into 8–10 large pieces. Combine fish, nuoc mam, pepper, and green onion (scallion), allow to marinate for 15 minutes.

Place water in a large saucepan and bring to the boil. Add the fish with its juices and the lemongrass. Reduce heat and simmer for 20 minutes. Meanwhile, combine tamarind pulp and boiling water, and allow to soak for 15 minutes. Strain mixture through a fine sieve and discard pulp.

Add the tamarind liquid, sugar, bamboo shoots, pineapple, and tomatoes to the pan. Simmer for 4–5 minutes until fish is tender.

Divide beansprouts between serving bowls and spoon over hot soup. Sprinkle over fresh herbs and deep fried shallots. Serve with lime wedges and sliced chili pepper on the side.

Hot-and-Sour Fish Soup

Ingredients

2½ lb firm-fleshed white fish (e.g. red snapper)

1½ tbsp nuoc mam (fish sauce)

¼ tsp white pepper

1 green onion (scallion), chopped

6 cups water

2 stalks lemongrass, cut into 2in lengths
and crushed lightly

2 oz/55 g tamarind pulp

¼ cup boiling water

1 tbsp sugar

¾ cup sliced bamboo shoots

1 cup sliced pineapple

2 tomatoes, cut into wedges

1 cup mixed Vietnamese herbs
(coriander,
bitter herb, Asian basil)

deep fried shallots

lime wedges, sliced chili pepper

Method

Peel the outer layers from the lemongrass stalks and chop the lower white bulbous parts into 3 pieces, discarding the fibrous tops. Shell shrimp, leaving tails attached and reserving the shells for the broth. Cut a slit along the back of each shrimp with a sharp knife and remove the thin black vein. Rinse the shrimp, then refrigerate until needed.

Heat the oil in a large saucepan. Fry the shrimp shells for 2–3 minutes, until pink Add the broth, garlic, ginger, lemongrass, lime rind, green chili pepper, and salt to taste. Bring to boil, then reduce heat, cover, and simmer for 20 minutes.

Strain the broth and return to the pan. Stir in the fish sauce and lime juice and bring to the boil. Add the shrimp, reduce the heat, and simmer for 3 minutes or until the shrimp turn pink and are cooked through. Season with pepper and serve garnished with red chili pepper and coriander (cilantro).

Thai Shrimp Soup

Ingredients

2 stalks lemongrass

1½ cups whole green shrimp, defrosted if frozen

1 tbsp vegetable oil

4 cups chicken broth

1 clove garlic, crushed

1in piece fresh root ginger, roughly chopped

2 limes, juice squeezed, rind of 1 grated

1 green chili pepper, deseeded and chopped

salt and black pepper

1 tbsp Thai fish sauce

1 red chili pepper, deseeded and sliced

2 tbsp chopped fresh coriander (cilantro) to garnish

Method

Pour the water into a large pot. Add the shin bones and beef. Bring to the boil and skim the surface. Turn heat to medium-low, partially cover, and simmer for two hours, skimming often, before adding remaining broth ingredients. Simmer another 90 minutes and remove from heat. Leave to cool.

Strain the broth through a fine sieve and discard bones, carrots, onion, and spices. Skim fat from broth. Cut the beef finely across the grain to paper thinness. Reserve.

Soak rice noodles in warm water about 20 minutes until soft, drain and reserve.

Return broth pot to heat to boil with fish sauce then reduce heat to very low. Fill a separate big pot three-quarters full of water and boil, add noodles and rinsed beansprouts. Continue cooking until noodles are tender but not mushy. Bean sprouts should retain some crispness.

Serve boiling broth first then drained noodles into 6 bowls, top equally with beef, raw onion rings, chopped green onions (scallions), and thin raw steak slices, which will par-cook in the bowls, and garnish with coriander and mint leaves.

Tip

The beef will be easiest to slice if semi-frozen in the freezer.

Diners help themselves to chili rings and lime wedges. This recipe can also be adapted for chicken which takes less time to cook.

Ingredients

Broth

2¼ lb shin beef bones

¾ lb/12 oz lean stewing beef

12 cups water

1 large brown, unpeeled onion, halved

3 medium pieces unpeeled ginger, sliced

pinch of salt

1 cinnamon stick

6 whole cloves

6 peppercorns

6 coriander seeds

4 whole star anise

2 un-peeled carrots, cut into chunks

Additions:

½ lb/8 oz thick steak in one piece

8 oz/225 g rice noodles

1 lb flat, thick, dried noodles

Beef Pho

2 tbsp fish sauce (nuoc mam)

1 brown onion, thinly sliced

3 green onions (scallions), finely chopped

½ cup beansprouts

½ cup fresh coriander (cilantro), torn into sprigs

½ cup vietnamese mint leaves, chopped

1 small red chili pepper, seeded and sliced into rings

2 limes cut into wedges

Method

Preheat broiler to high.

Place mushrooms and wine in a non-reactive saucepan over a medium heat. Bring to the boil. Cook, stirring occasionally, for 2—3 minutes or until mushrooms are tender. Using a slotted spoon, remove mushrooms from wine. Drain well. Set aside. Reserve cooking liquid.

Place chili pepper, black pepper, and lime rind in a mortar and grind with the pestle to make a coarse paste. Rub paste over beef. Broil for 1—2 minutes on each side, or until just browned – the beef should be very rare. Remove beef from grill. Rest for 5 minutes. Cut, across the grain, into very thin slices. Set aside.

Stir sugar, broth, lime juice, and fish sauce into reserved cooking liquid. Place over a medium heat. Bring to the boil. Remove from heat.

Add meat. Turn to coat. Transfer meat mixture to a bowl. Add green onions, basil, mint, and reserved mushrooms. Toss to combine.

To serve, pile salad onto a serving platter. Scatter with coriander and peanuts. Accompany with steamed jasmine rice.

Warm Thai Beef and Mushroom Salad

Ingredients

2 cups shiitake mushrooms, trimmed and quartered

2 cups oyster mushrooms, trimmed and quartered

½ cup rice wine (mirin) or dry white wine

1 small fresh red chili pepper, chopped

2 tsp freshly ground black pepper

1 tsp grated lime rind

1¼ lb lean beef steak (e.g. fillet, topside or round), trimmed of visible fat

1 tsp sugar

1/4 cup low-sodium chicken or vegetable broth

1 lime, juice squeezed

2 tbsp fish sauce

2 green onions or shallots, thinly sliced

1 cup fresh Thai or sweet basil leaves

2 tbsp fresh mint leaves

2 tbsp chopped fresh coriander

2 tbsp chopped dry roasted unsalted cashews or peanuts

Method

Peel the mangoes and slice the flesh into thin strips. Run a vegetable peeler down the length of the cucumber to form long ribbons and put in a bowl with the bell pepper, mint, and coriander. Toss, cover, and refrigerate while preparing the rest of the salad.

Put the lime juice, ginger, fish sauce, sweet chili sauce, and palm sugar in a jug and whisk to combine.

Preheat a broiler, lightly brush the fish fillets with the peanut oil and cook over a high heat for 3–4 minutes on each side or until cooked. Place some of the salad on each plate and top with fish fillets.

Drizzle the dressing over the fish and salad. Serve sprinkled with peanuts.

Thai Fish and Mango Salad

Ingredients

2 small mangoes

2 small cucumbers

1 red bell pepper, roasted, peeled and cut into thin strips

2 tbsp fresh mint sprigs

2 tbsp fresh coriander sprigs

⅓ cup lime juice

1 tsp fresh ginger, grated

2 tbsp fish sauce

2 tbsp sweet chili sauce

1 tbsp grated light palm sugar or brown sugar

4 fillets (about ½ lb/9oz each) white fish

1 tbsp peanut oil

2 tbsp unsalted peanuts, roughly chopped

Method

Peel the outer layer from the lemongrass and chop the lower white bulbous part, discarding the fibrous top. Blend to a paste with the onion, garlic, coriander (cilantro), turmeric, lemon juice, and 1 tsp of salt in a food processor. Alternatively, grind the lemongrass, onion, and garlic with a pestle and mortar, then mix in the other ingredients.

Place the chicken in a non-reactive bowl and coat with the paste. Cover and marinate in the fridge for 2 hours, or overnight. If using wooden skewers, soak them in water for 10 minutes.

To make the satay sauce, blend the onion and garlic to a paste in a food processor or grind with a pestle and mortar. Heat the oil in a heavy-based saucepan and fry the paste for 5 minutes, stirring. Mix in the chilipowder, then the remaining sauce ingredients. Bring to the boil, stirring, then simmer for 10 minutes.

Preheat the broiler to high. Thread the chicken onto 8 skewers. Broil for 10 minutes, turning once, until cooked. Serve with the cucumber and satay sauce.

Chicken Satays

Ingredients

1 stalk lemongrass

1 onion, chopped

1 clove garlic, chopped

2 tsp ground coriander (cilantro)

1 tsp turmeric

½ lemon, juice squeezed

salt and black pepper

3 skinless, boneless chicken breasts, cut into

½ in cubes

½ cucumber, pared into ribbons with

a vegetable peeler, to serve

For the satay sauce

1 small onion, chopped

1 clove garlic, chopped

1 tbsp peanut oil

1 tsp chili powder

⅔ cup coconut milk

⅓ cup/3 oz roasted salted peanuts,

finely ground

1 tbsp soft dark brown sugar

1 tbsp fresh lemon juice

Method

To make batter, place flour, cornstarch, and chili powder in a bowl, mix to combine, and make a well in the center. Whisk in egg and water and beat until smooth. Add ice cubes

Heat oil in a deep saucepan until a cube of bread dropped in browns in 50 seconds.

Dip shrimp, snow peas, eggplant (aubergine) and broccoli florets in batter and deep-fry a few at a time for 3–4 minutes or until golden and crisp. Serve immediately.

Serving suggestion: All that is needed to make this a complete meal is a variety of purchased dipping sauces, chutneys, relishes, and a tossed green salad.

Chili Tempura

Ingredients

vegetable oil for deep-frying

1lb uncooked large shrimp, peeled and deveined, tails left intact

12 snow peas (mangetout), trimmed

1 eggplant (aubergine), cut into thin slices

1 small head broccoli, broken into small florets

Tempura Batter

¼ cup self-rising flour

½ cup cornstarch

1 teaspoon chili powder

1 egg, lightly beaten

1 cup iced water

4 ice cubes

Method

Place the chicken in a glass bowl, mix marinade ingredients together and pour over chicken. Cover and place in refrigerator to marinate for several hours or overnight.

Thread 2 tenderloins onto each skewer, using a weaving motion. Heat barbecue or electric grill to medium-high. Grease grill bars or griddle lightly with oil.

Place skewers in a row, and cook for 2 minutes on each side, brushing with marinade as they cook, and when turned. Remove to a large serving platter. Serve immediately as finger food.

Chicken Yakitori

Ingredients

1lb chicken breasts

Marinade

¼ cup teriyaki sauce

¼ cup honey

1 garlic clove, crushed

¼ tsp ginger, ground

small bamboo skewers, soaked

oil for greasing

Method

Peel the outer layers from the lemon grass stalks and finely chop the lower white bulbous parts, discarding the fibrous tops. Put the chicken cubes into a large bowl, add the lemongrass and sesame oil, and toss to coat the chicken. Cover and refrigerate for at least 2 hours, or overnight.

Heat a wok or large, heavy-based frying pan, then add the vegetable oil. Add the chicken with its marinade and stir-fry for 5 minutes or until the chicken meat is firm.

Add the red pepper, peanuts, fish sauce, soy sauce, sugar, and salt to taste. Stir-fry for another 5 minutes or until the chicken and pepper are cooked. Sprinkle with the green onions (scallions) just before serving.

Stir-fried Lemongrass Chicken

Ingredients

4 stalks lemon grass

1 lb skinless boneless chicken breasts, cut into 1in cubes

1 tsp sesame oil

2 tbsp vegetable oil

1 red bell pepper, deseeded and chopped

2 tbsp roasted salted peanuts, roughly chopped

1 tbsp soy sauce

1 tbsp fish sauce

½ tbsp sugar

salt

2 green onions (scallions), chopped

lemon juice

Method

Heat oil and garlic together in a wok over a medium heat, increase heat to high, add beef and stir-fry for 3 minutes, or until beef turns color.

Add beans, lime leaves, sugar, soy, and fish sauces, and stir-fry for 2 minutes or until beans turn color.

Stir in coriander (cilantro) and serve immediately.

Ingredients

2 tsp vegetable oil

2 cloves garlic, crushed

1 lb topside or round steak, cut into thin strips

¼ lb/6 oz snake (yard-long) or green beans, cut into 4 in lengths

2 kaffir lime leaves, shredded

2 tsp brown sugar

2 tbsp light soy sauce

1 tbsp Thai fish sauce (nam pla)

2 tbsp coriander (cilantro) leaves

Beef and Bean Stir-fry

Tip

Kaffir limes are a popular Thai ingredient. Both the fruit
and the leaves have a distinctive flavor and fragrance
and are used extensively in cooking.
The leaves are available dried, frozen, or fresh from
oriental grocery stores and some green grocers.
If kaffir lime leaves are unavailable a little finely grated lime
rind can be used instead.

Method

Crush or pound ingredients for the paste in a mortar with a pestle or in a food processor.

Heat oil in a large saucepan. Add chicken and cook until golden. Remove chicken and set aside.

Add onions and cook for 3−4 minutes or until brown. Add paste and cook for 1−2 minutes. Add coriander, cumin, and laos powder and cook until aromatic.

Add coconut cream, milk, kaffir lime leaves, and chicken. Bring to the boil, reduce heat and simmer for 20−30 minutes or until chicken is tender and liquid has reduced.

Chicken in Coconut Milk

Ingredients

Paste

2 cloves garlic

2 tsp chopped ginger

1 tsp terasi (shrimp paste)

3 candlenuts (or macadamias or almonds)

1 small red chili, deseeded

½ tsp salt

2 tbsp peanut oil

8 chicken pieces

2 onions, sliced

2 tsp ground coriander

1 tsp ground cumin

pinch of laos powder (or ginger powder)

1½ cups creamed coconut

1½ cups coconut milk

2 kaffir lime leaves, thinly sliced

Method

Grind or pound ingredients for paste in a mortar with a pestle or in a food processor. If using a food processor you may need to add a little oil.

Heat oil in a wok or skillet. Add paste and cook for 1–2 minutes. Add broth and lemongrass. Bring to the boil.

Add beans and cook for 8–10 minutes or until beans are tender.

Spicy Long Beans

Ingredients

Paste

4 small red chili peppers, deseeded and sliced

2 shallots, chopped

2 tsp chopped ginger

2 tsp chopped garlic

2 tsp peanut oil

1 cup chicken broth

1 stalk lemongrass, bruised

1 cup runner beans, trimmed

Method

Soak mushrooms in hot water for 40 minutes. Remove stalks and discard.
Cut green onions (scallions) into 1½in pieces. Seed green pepper and chili and cut into pieces. Combine marinade ingredients.

Cut spare ribs into large bite-sized pieces and marinate 30 minutes. Deep-fry until brown. Remove from heat. Sauté green onions (scallions) and mushrooms in oil, return ribs to pan with ½ tsp salt, sugar, dark soy sauce, ⅓ cup water and stir fry. Add bell pepper, chili, and combined sauce ingredients.

Mix well, stirring, until the chili pepper just starts to lose its crispness.
Serve on a pre-heated heavy-metal grill pan so meat sizzles. Serve garnished with mint sprigs.

Sizzling Spare Ribs

Ingredients

1lb pork or beef spare ribs

8 dried mushrooms, 2 green onions (scallions)

1 green bell pepper, 1 red chili

½ tsp salt, ½ tsp sugar

1 tsp dark soy

⅓ cup water, oil for frying

Marinade

½ tsp salt, ½ tsp dry sherry

1 tbsp light soy sauce

2 tsp cornstarch

Sauce

½ tsp cornstarch, dash of sesame oil

ground black pepper, 1½ tbsp fish sauce,

mint leaves for garnish

Method

In a heavy-based pan, heat oil, add pork cubes, and turn until brown. Add garlic and onion and cook until the slices separate into rings and are transparent. Remove from heat.

In a separate saucepan, mix sugar with water and stir over low heat until sugar dissolves. Bring to boil then reduce heat and simmer, still stirring, until liquid is golden. Take pot off heat and carefully add fish sauce and lime juice which will spatter. Return to heat, stirring quickly to remove any lumps and until the sauce reduces a little.

Quickly return pork, garlic, and onions to reheat, add chili spice then caramel. Cook for 1 minute, stirring until combined. Transfer to serving dish and sprinkle green onions (scallions) on top.

Tip

Pour boiling water immediately into pot in which caramel has cooked
or the caramel will stick fast and be very difficult to remove.

Ingredients

1½ lb pork, cubed

2 medium onions, sliced

⅓ cup sugar

¾ cup water

1½ tbsp fish sauce

1½ tbsp lime juice

½ tsp salt

Caramelized Pork

1 seeded red chili pepper, sliced and chopped

½ tsp five spice powder

2 garlic cloves, minced

oil for frying

2 green onions (scallions), chopped, for garnish

Method

Place chicken in a ceramic or glass dish and set aside.

Place chili peppers, garlic, coriander roots, lemongrass, lime juice, and soy sauce in a food processor and process to make paste. Mix paste with coconut cream and pour this over chicken. Marinate for 1 hour.

Drain chicken and reserve marinade. Cook chicken over a slow charcoal or gas barbecue or under a preheated broiler on low, brushing frequently with reserved marinade, for 25–30 minutes or until chicken is tender. Serve with chili sauce.

Method

Place garlic, coriander, and black peppercorns in a food processor and process to make a paste. Coat chicken with garlic paste and marinate for 1 hour.

Heat oil in a wok or frying pan over a high heat until a cube of bread dropped in browns in 60 seconds. Deep-fry the chicken, a few pieces at a time, for 2 minutes or until golden and tender. Drain on absorbent kitchen paper.

Deep-fry basil and mint until crisp, then drain and place on a serving plate. Top with chicken and serve with chili sauce.

Chargrilled Chicken
Chicken with Garlic and Pepper

Chargrilled chicken

2¼ lb chicken pieces

4 fresh red chili peppers, chopped

4 cloves garlic, chopped

2 tbsp coriander leaves, chopped

2 stalks fresh lemongrass, chopped,

or 1 tsp dried lemongrass soaked

in hot water until soft

3 tbsp lime juice

2 tbsp light soy sauce

1 cup coconut cream

1 tbsp sweet chili sauce

Chicken with Garlic and Pepper

4 cloves garlic

3 fresh coriander sprigs

1 tsp crushed black peppercorns

1¼ lb chicken breast fillets,

cut into 1¼ in cubes

vegetable oil for deep-frying

2 tbsp fresh basil leaves

2 tbsp fresh mint leaves

1 tbsp sweet chili sauce

Method

Place chicken under a hot broiler and cook for two minutes each side. Heat teriyaki sauce in a large frying pan. Place chicken into pan and cook for a further two minutes on each side. Slice each chicken fillet into ½ in strips. Arrange carefully onto warmed serving plate.

Combine vegetables with sugar, light soy sauce, and sesame oil. Stir fry over a high heat for 1–2 minutes.

Arrange vegetables beside the chicken, sprinkle with sesame seeds and serve.

TERIYAKI SAUCE

Combine all ingredients in a saucepan. Heat until sugar has dissolved. Remove from heat and allow to cool.

Makes 3¾ cups

Teriyaki Chicken with Kinpira Vegetables

Ingredients

4 chicken breast fillets

1 cup teriyaki sauce

4 green asparagus, cut into quarters

4 white asparagus, cut into quarters

4 baby carrots, cut into quarters lengthwise

4 baby corn, cut into quarters lengthwise

1 tbsp sugar

1 tbsp light soy sauce

2 tsp sesame oil

2 tsp white sesame seeds

Teriyaki Sauce

1¾ cups mirin

1½ cups soy sauce

3½ fl oz saké

⅓ cup sugar

Method

Preheat oven to 425°F

Combine soy sauce, tamarind, oil, ginger, garlic, and coriander. Pour marinade over duck and leave to marinate for 2–3 hours.

Heat oil in a skillet. Add duck and cook for 1–2 minutes or until golden and crisp. Place duck on a rack over a roasting pan and cook for 15–18 minutes. Slice duck and serve with salad greens.

Crispy Fried Duck

Ingredients

2 tbsp soy sauce

1 tbsp tamarind concentrate

1 tbsp peanut oil

1 tsp grated ginger

1 clove garlic crushed

4 duck breasts

1 tsp ground coriander

1/4 cup peanut oil, for frying

Method

Crush or pound the shallots, garlic and shrimp paste with the peanut oil in a mortar with pestle or in a food processor.

Heat the frying oil in a wok or skillet. Stir-fry the beef for 3–4 minutes or until browned. Add the lombok chili peppers and ketjap manis. Heat the broth and dissolve the tamarind concentrate in it. Add this to the wok with the shallot-and-shrimp paste. Reduce the heat,cover the pan and simmer for around 10 minutes. Add the cubed eggplant and green onions and cook for another 5–6 minutes until the meat is well cooked and has absorbed most of the liquid of the sauce.

Ingredients

2 shallots, minced

2 garlic cloves, minced

½ tsp terasi (shrimp paste)

2 tsp peanut oil

1 tbsp oil for frying

1lb/10oz rump steak, diced

Beef in Tamarind

Paste

1 tbsp ketjap manis (sweet soy sauce)

1 tbsp tamarind concentrate

½–¾ cup beef broth

1 eggplant, diced

2 green onions, sliced

Method

Place a fish fillet or cutlet in the center of each banana leaf. Top fish with a little each of the garlic, ginger, and lime leaves, then fold over banana leaves to enclose. Place packages over a charcoal barbecue or bake in the oven for 15–20 minutes or until fish flakes when tested with a fork.

To make sauce, place mango, shallots, chili peppers, sugar, water, and fish sauce in a saucepan and cook, stirring, over a low heat for 4–5 minutes or until sauce is heated through.

To serve, place packages on serving plates, cut open to expose fish and serve with sauce.

Method

Make diagonal slashes along both sides of the fish.

Place chopped chili peppers, coriander roots, garlic, and black peppercorns in a food processor and process to make a paste. Spread mixture over both sides of fish and marinate for 30 minutes.

To make sauce, place sugar, sliced chili peppers, shallots, vinegar, and water in a saucepan and cook, stirring, over a low heat until sugar dissolves.Bring mixture to simmering and simmer, stirring occasionally, for 4 minutes or until sauce thickens.

Heat vegetable oil in a wok or deep-frying pan until a cube of bread dropped in browns in 50 seconds. Cook fish, one at a time, for 2 minutes each side or until crisp and flesh flakes when tested with a fork. Drain on absorbent kitchen paper. Serve with chili pepper sauce. Serves 6

Ingredients

4 x ¼ lb/6 oz firm fish fillets or cutlets

4 pieces banana leaf, blanched

3 cloves garlic, sliced

1 tbsp shredded fresh ginger

2 kaffir lime leaves, shredded

Green mango sauce

½ small green (unripe) mango, flesh grated

3 red or golden shallots, chopped

2 fresh red chili peppers, sliced

1 tbsp brown sugar

¼ cup water

1 tbsp Thai fish sauce (nam pla)

Fish with Green Mango Sauce
Deep-fried Chili Pepper Fish

Deep-fried chili pepper fish

2 x 1 lb whole fish such as bream, snapper, whiting,

sea perch, cleaned

4 fresh red chili peppers, chopped

4 fresh coriander roots

3 cloves garlic, crushed

vegetable oil for deep-frying

red pepper sauce

⅔ cup sugar

8 fresh red chili peppers, sliced

4 red or golden shallots, sliced

⅓ cup coconut vinegar

⅓ cup water

1 tsp crushed black peppercorns

Method

Combine garlic, ginger, lemongrass, ketjap manis, soy sauce, sambal oelek, and sesame oil in a shallow dish.

Add chicken and coat well in marinade. Leave to marinate for 1–2 hours.

Heat oil in a wok or skillet. Add chicken, reserving the marinade, and stir-fry for 4–5 minutes or until golden.

Add marinade and snow peas and bamboo shoots and stir-fry for 2–3 minutes or until snow peas are cooked.

Add a little water if the sauce becomes too thick.

Ingredients

2 cloves garlic, crushed

2 tsp ginger, chopped

1 stalk lemongrass, finely chopped

1 tbsp ketjap manis (sweet soy sauce)

1 tsp sambal oelek (or chili paste)

2 tsp sesame oil

Marinated Chicken with Snow Peas

1¼ lb chicken breasts, halved

1 tbsp peanut oil

⅔ cup snow peas, trimmed and halved

1 cup canned bamboo shoots, drained

Method

Preheat oven to 40°F

Make two diagonal cuts on each side of the fish. Brush fish with oil and lime juice. Season with salt and place slices of lime in the fish. Wrap fish in nonstick baking paper or aluminum foil and place in a roasting pan. Bake in for 30–40 minutes or until cooked.

Heat oil in a small saucepan. Add garlic, ginger, chili pepper, and shallots and cook for 1–2 minutes. Add soy sauce, ketjap manis, and water and cook for 2–3 minutes. When fish is baked, transfer to a large serving platter and coat it with the sauce.

Baked Fish with Spicy Soy Sauce

Ingredients

1 lb /12oz whole red snapper

2 tsp peanut oil

1 tbsp lime juice

pinch salt

Fish Sauce

2 tsp peanut oil

2 garlic cloves, crushed

2 tsp grated ginger

1 small red chili pepper, deseeded and sliced

4 green onions, sliced

2 tbsp soy sauce

1 tbsp ketjap manis (sweet soy sauce)

½ cup water

Method

Prepare banana leaf by cutting into 6in squares. Line each banana leaf with nonstick baking paper.

Combine fish, shallots, garlic, ginger, lime juice, and egg in a food processor. Process until mixture coheres into a paste.

Divide mixture evenly into 4 and place one portion in the center of each banana leaf, patting it down into a rectangle. Wrap the fish in the nonstick baking paper to make a package, seam side downward, and then fold the banana leaf the same way. Secure with cocktail sticks.

Cook the packages in a bamboo steamer for 10–15 minutes.

Serve fish with wedges of lime.

Ingredients

4 large pieces banana leaf

1 lb /10oz boneless white fish fillets

2 shallots, minced

2 garlic cloves, minced

2 tsp chopped ginger

2 tbsp lime juice

1 egg, beaten

lime wedges to garnish

Fish in Banana Leaves

5 tbsp coconut milk

1 lime, sliced

4 small chili peppers, finely chopped

nonstick baking paper, cocktail stick

Method

Grind or pound ingredients for the paste in a mortar with a pestle or in a food processor. Brush the paste over fish fillets.

Heat the oil in a large skillet. Add fish fillets and fry for 1–2 minutes on each side. Add coconut milk, sugar, and lime juice and simmer 2–3 minutes.

Serve fish topped with green onions.

Fried Fish

Ingredients

1 tbsp peanut oil

4 boneless fish fillets

½–¾ cup coconut milk

1 tsp palm sugar or brown sugar

1 tbsp lime juice

4 green onions, sliced

Boemboe paste

2 garlic cloves, chopped

2 tsp chopped ginger

1 stalk lemongrass, sliced

2 medium chili peppers, deseeded and sliced

2 candlenuts (or macadamias or almonds)

½ tsp ground turmeric (or ground ginger)

2 tsp peanut oil

Method

Prepare dipping sauce by mixing shrimp paste, a little extra oil, fish sauce, and sugar. Boil and add more sugar if desired.

Season fish with salt and pepper and cut into 1in pieces. In a heavy-based pan, heat oil, add fish, turmeric, and ginger. Turn gently and just before fish is done, add green onions (scallions), dill, and peanuts. Arrange lettuce and mint on a bed of rice and serve with the fish. Serve with dipping sauce.

Hanoi-Style Fried Fish

Ingredients

1lb boneless fish fillets

4 tsp grated turmeric

2 tbsp shrimp paste

¼ cup soy bean oil

¼ cup peanut oil

½ cup fresh dill, chopped

4 green onions (scallions), chopped

1 heaping tsp ginger, grated

¼ cup fish sauce

1 tbsp sugar

2 tbsp crushed peanuts

salt and pepper

lettuce, mint leaves and cooked rice, to serve

Method

Cook noodles following package directions. Drain noodles and reserve them.

Heat the oil in a wok. Add shallots and cook until golden. Add chicken and garlic and stir-fry for 2 minutes. Add carrots and stir-fry for a further 2 minutes.

Add cabbage and ketjap manis and continue to cook until cabbage is wilted.

Add chicken broth, noodles, beansprouts, and green onions. Stir fry until heated through.

Fried Noodles

Ingredients

7 oz/200 g egg noodles or vermicelli

1 tbsp peanut oil

1¼ lb chicken thighs, boned and diced

4 shallots, sliced

2 garlic cloves, crushed

1 carrot, peeled and finely sliced

2 cup Chinese (Napa) cabbage, shredded

2 tbsp ketjap manis (sweet soy sauce)

⅓ cup chicken broth

1 cup beansprouts

4 green onions (scallions), sliced

Method

Heat the oil in a wok or skillet. Add the tofu and cook until golden and crisp. Remove and set aside.

Heat the peanut oil and add ginger and chili peppers. Stir-fry for 1–2 minutes. Add soy sauce, water, sugar, tofu, and snow peas. Stir-fry for 2–3 minutes or until snow peas are tender. Stir in the beansprouts and serve.

Fried Bean Curd in Soy Sauce

Ingredients

½ cup vegetable oil for frying

1 cup tofu, diced

2 tsp peanut oil

2 tsp grated ginger

2 medium chili peppers, deseeded and sliced

¼ cup soy sauce

1–2 tbsp water

2 tsp palm sugar or brown sugar

1 cup snow peas, trimmed and halved

1 cup beansprouts, trimmed

Method

Heat butter or oil in a wok or heavy saucepan, add all seasoning ingredients, and sauté for 2–3 minutes. Add the chicken and continue sautéing for 3 minutes over high heat.

Add chicken broth and salt, and simmer until chicken is tender. Strain the brother and reserve the chicken pieces. Place rice in a rice-cooker or heavy pot, add 2½ cups of the reserved chicken broth, and bring to the boil. Cover the pan and simmer until the rice is almost cooked and the liquid absorbed. Add the diced chicken and cook over low heat until the rice is thoroughly cooked.

Serve on a platter garnished with fried shallots and pineapple pieces.

Ingredients

2 tbsp butter or oil

1¼ lb boneless chicken, cut in ½ in cubes

3 cups chicken broth

1 tsp salt

2 cups long-grain rice, washed and drained

½ small pineapple, peeled and cut into small pieces

13 shallots, peeled and minced

7 garlic cloves, peeled and minced

Seasoning

1in ginger, peeled and chopped

1 tsp coriander

½ tsp white peppercorns

½ tsp cumin seed

Chicken and Rice with Pineapple

a little freshly grated nutmeg

3 in cinnamon stick

4 cardamom pods, bruised

2 cloves

1 piece lemongrass, bruised

Method

Combine the lime juice with the rice wine and crushed garlic. Marinate the bay scallops for 15 minutes. Set aside.

While the scallops are marinating, grate the ginger, slice the spring (green) onions, and mushrooms, and dice the red bell pepper. Heat the sesame oil in a hot wok or large skillet until almost smoking.

To the wok, add the ginger, spring (green) onions, mushrooms, and red bell pepper. Stir-fry for about 3 minutes, until the ginger has become fragrant. Add the scallops and marinade. Continue stir-frying for another 3 minutes, until scallops have become opaque, mixing the wok ingredients together well. Add the soy sauce; mix thoroughly. Pepper to taste.

Dilute the cornstarch with water and pour the liquid into the wok. Cook for another minute or two or until the sauce has thickened and become smooth.

Serve immediately with steamed white rice.

Ginger Scallop Stir-Fry

Ingredients

2 tbsp fresh lime juice

2 tbsp rice wine

1 garlic clove, crushed

½ lb/8 oz scallops

1 tbsp sesame oil

2 tsp ginger, finely grated

4 spring (green) onions, cut diagonally into ½-inch lengths

½ red bell pepper, diced

3 oz button mushrooms, sliced

2 tsp soy sauce

pinch of black pepper, 1 tsp cornstarch

2 tbsp water

Method

Slice steak into thin strips about 2in long. Separate cauliflower into flowerets then divide into two. Drain liquid from mushrooms, measure 1/2 cup and mix with cornstarch, 1 tbsp fish sauce, and oyster sauce. Peel and finely chop garlic. Cut onion lengthwise into eighths.

Pour 1 tbsp fish sauce over sliced meat and grind pepper over it. Turn and leave to stand for 20 minutes.

Heat the oil in a frying pan, add garlic and onion, and stir-fry until onion separates and softens. Add cauliflower and mushrooms. Cover, reduce heat, and cook for 4 minutes. Add meat and cook until meat is cooked to your liking. Stir in liquid mixture. Continue stirring till sauce thickens. On serving plate and garnish with coriander sprigs.

Ingredients

1 cup fresh button mushrooms, whole

1½ tsp cornstarch

½ cup water or broth

2 tbsp fish sauce

1 tsp sugar

1 tsp oyster sauce

Beef, Cauliflower, and Mushroom Stir-fry

½ lb/8 oz steak

¼ cauliflower

vegetable oil

3 garlic cloves

1 medium onion

black pepper, ground

coriander sprigs, to garnish

Method

Combine oil, lime juice, soy sauce, garlic, coriander and cumin. Place lamb cutlets in a dish. Pour marinade over them and marinate for 2–3 hours.

Cook lamb cutlets on a barbecue griddle, or under the broiler for 8–10 minutes, basting and turning from time to time.

Serve with nasi goreng and peanut sauce.

Barbecued Lamb Cutlets

Ingredients

2 tbsp peanut oil

¼ cup lime juice

1 tbsp soy sauce

2 garlic cloves, crushed

1 tsp ground coriander

1 tsp ground cumin

8 lamb cutlets

nasi goreng and peanut sauce , to serve

Method

Heat oil in a wok or frying pan over a medium heat, add garlic and black peppercorns and stir-fry for 1 minute. Add pork and stir-fry for 3 minutes or until brown.

Add bok choy, coriander (cilantro), sugar, soy sauce, and lime juice, and stir-fry for 3–4 minutes or until pork and bok choy are tender.

Method

Place curry paste in wok and cook, stirring, over a high heat for 2 minutes or until fragrant. Add onions and cook for 2 minutes longer or until onions are soft. Remove from pan and set aside.

Heat oil in wok, add pork and stir-fry for 3 minutes or until brown. Remove pork from pan and set aside.

Add pumpkin, lime leaves, sugar, coconut milk, and fish sauce to pan, bring to simmering and simmer for 2 minutes. Stir in curry paste mixture and simmer for 5 minutes longer. Return pork to pan and cook for 2 minutes or until heated.

Tip

Bok choy is also known as Chinese cabbage, bock choy, and pak choi. It varies in length from 4–12in. For this recipe, the smaller variety is used. It has a mild, cabbage-like flavor. Ordinary cabbage could be used for this recipe.

Pork in Garlic Pepper; Pork and Pumpkin Stir-fry

Pork and Pumpkin Stir-fry

Ingredients

2 tbsp Thai red curry paste

2 onions, cut into thin wedges, layers separated

2 tsp vegetable oi

1 lb lean pork strips

1 lb peeled butternut pumpkin (squash), cut into 3⁄4 in cubes

4 kaffir lime leaves, shredded

1 tbsp palm or brown sugar

2 cups coconut milk

1 tbsp Thai fish sauce (nam pla)

Ingredients

2 tsp vegetable oil

4 cloves garlic, sliced

1 tbsp crushed black peppercorns

1 lb lean pork strips

1 lb bok choy (Chinese greens), chopped

4 tbsp fresh coriander (cilantro) leaves

2 tbsp palm or brown sugar

2 tbsp light soy sauce

2 tbsp lime juice

Method

Part-freeze steak to make it easier to cut each piece into 2 thin slices, making four slices. Place steak on a plate and cut into four slices. Spread each with bell pepper, garlic, and 1 tbsp oil. Turn steak to marinate it, cover, and refrigerate for 45 minutes.

Pour 2½ tbsp oil into a heavy-based pan, ensuring the based is coated. Separate the noodles with hands. Heat oil to medium, add noodles and press them in and down with hands and spatula to fit the pan. Heat until noodles are golden and crisp. Cook until browned then leave it in the pan for about 15 minutes as it will break up.

Loosen edges and base of pancake gently. Place a large plate over the pan and quickly invert the pan to settle the pancake on the plate. Gently slide the pancake back into the pan, uncooked side down and continue cooking 5 to 10 minutes. Return pancake to plate in the same manner and keep warm in low oven.

In same pan, heat 2½ tbsp oil until smoking, add meat and bell pepper mix and sear quickly on both sides, not overcooking. Mix sugar, fish sauce, broth and cornstarch till smooth and add to steak. Turn meat to absorb flavors, remove it and stir sauce rapidly until thick, returning steak briefly to coat with sauce.

Serve steak and sauce on top of pancake and cut into 4 or 8 if presenting as an entree. Top with sauce and garnish with chopped green onions (scallions).

Ingredients

¾ lb/11 oz fillet steak

6 tbsp vegetable oil

½ red bell pepper, deseeded and sliced

3 tsp garlic, minced

½ tsp ground black pepper

Noodle Pancake with Garlic Beef

14 oz/400 g fresh, soft noodles

2 tsp cornstarch

2 tsp/ fish sauce

1 tbsp sugar

½ cup beef broth

2 green onions (scallions) chopped

Method

Heat oil in a large saucepan. Add onion and cook for 2–3 minutes or until soft.

Add garlic, terasi, and candlenuts and cook for 1 minute.

Add coconut milk, chicken broth, sambal oelek, and lemongrass.

Bring to the boil. Add broccoli and cauliflower. Cover and simmer for 4 minutes.

Add zucchini and beans and continue to cook for 3–4 minutes or until vegetables are barely tender.

Remove lemongrass just before serving.

Vegetables in Coconut Milk

Ingredients

1 tbsp peanut oil

1 onion, sliced

2 cloves garlic, crushed

1 tsp terasi (shrimp paste), crushed

2 candlenuts, crushed

½ cup coconut milk

1 cup chicken broth

1 tsp sambal oelek

1 stalk lemongrass, bruised

1 head broccoli, cut into flowerets

¼ cauliflower, cut into flowerets

1 large zucchini, halved and sliced

⅔ cup green beans, sliced

Method

Rinse chickens inside and out and pat dry with paper towels. Make deep gashes in thighs and on each side of breast. Pin back the wings.

Combine tandoori curry paste, yogurt, lemon juice, and melted butter. Place chickens in a stainless steel or other non-reactive bowl and spread the mixture all over, rubbing well into the gashes. Cover and refrigerate for 12 or more hours. Place chickens on a roasting rack in a baking dish and spoon any remaining marinade over chickens.

Preheat the oven to 370°F and cook for 1 hour. Baste with pan juices during cooking. When cooked, cover with foil and rest for 10 minutes before serving. Arrange crisp lettuce leaves on a large serving platter and cover with onion rings. Cut chicken into portions and place on the platter. Garnish with tomato wedges and lemon slices.

Ingredients

2 x 2 lbs roasting chickens

3 tbsp tandoori curry paste

1 scant cup plain yogurt

2 tbsp lemon juice

2 tbsp melted butter

lettuce, onion rings, tomato and lemon for serving

Tandoori Chicken

Tip

Chickens portions may be used instead
of whole chickens. Turn frequently while
they are roasting.

Method

Place noodles in a bowl and pour boiling water to cover over them. If using fresh noodles soak for 2 minutes; if using dried noodles soak for 5-6 minutes or until soft. Drain well and set aside.

Heat oil in a frying pan or wok over a high heat, add shallots, chili peppers, and ginger and stir-fry for 1 minute. Add chicken and shrimp, and stir-fry for 4 minutes or until cooked.

Add noodles, peanuts, sugar, lime juice, and fish and soy sauces and stir-fry for 4 minutes or until heated through. Stir in tofu, beansprouts, coriander (cilantro), and mint and cook for 1–2 minutes or until heated through. Serve with lime wedges.

Ingredients

10 oz/315 g fresh or dried rice noodles

2 tsp vegetable oil

4 red or golden shallots, chopped

3 fresh red chili peppers, chopped

2 tbsp shredded fresh ginger

1 cup boneless chicken breast fillets, chopped

1 cup raw shrimp, shelled and deveined

2 tbsp roasted peanuts, chopped

1 tbsp sugar

Pad Thai

4 tbsp lime juice

3 tbsp fish sauce

2 tbsp light soy sauce

½ cup tofu, chopped

¼ cup bean sprouts

4 tbsp fresh coriander (cilantro)
leaves

3 tbsp fresh mint leaves

lime wedges to serve

Method

Arrange sliced beef decoratively on a plate. Place all vegetables and tofu on another platter.

Heat beef fat in a sukiyaki pan (or other heavy-based frying pan) on the serving table. Cook some of each ingredient while adding a little sukiyaki sauce to the pan. Cook for only a few minutes before serving. Guests may choose to dip the cooked ingredients into the beaten egg before eating.

Continue to cook remaining ingredients while adding a little more sukiyaki sauce to the pan as required.

To make Sukyaki Sauce: Place all ingredients in a saucepan and heat until sugar has dissolved.

Sukiyaki

Ingredients

¼ lb/4 oz marbled porterhouse steak

¼ lb/3½ oz Chinese cabbage

½ onion, sliced

2 shiitake mushrooms

4 pieces sliced carrot, 8 cubes tofu

4 spring (green) onions

2 oz/50 g syungiku, 1 oz/30 g beef fat

2 eggs, beaten

Sukiyaki Sauce

1¼ cups mirin

1¼ cups soy sauce

½ cup saké,

½ cup sugar

⅓ cup suiji

Method

To make the caramel, dissolve the sugar over low heat, in a small, heavy-based pan, swirling constantly until the sugar becomes golden. Stir in hot water carefully as the mixture will splatter. Quickly stir to dissolve any lumps and boil about 2 minutes until liquid and dark brown but not burned.

Grease a 6-cup soufflé dish with butter or margarine and pour the caramel into it. Tilt dish to ensure caramel coats the base.

To make the custard, beat eggs and vanilla in a large bowl. Combine coconut milk and milk with sugar in a saucepan and cook over low heat until sugar dissolves. Remove from stove and beat quickly into eggs and vanilla so eggs do not curdle. Sieve custard only if it is lumpy. Pour slowly into soufflé dish on top of caramel.

Pre-heat oven to 325°F In the base of a large roasting pan, place two layers of paper toweling, then the soufflé dish before pouring hot water into the roasting pan to come half-way up the soufflé dish. Bake in the center of the oven for about 50 minutes or until a knife inserted into custard is clean when removed. Do not allow water to boil. Remove soufflé dish. Cool in a pan of cold water. Chill, covered with plastic wrap, preferably overnight.

To serve, run a knife round the inside edge of the soufflé dish and place a dinner plate on top. In a quick movement, invert the dish and the crème caramel will unmold onto the plate. Serve alone or with whipped cream. Place a mint sprig in the center to garnish.

Ingredients

Caramel

¼ cup sugar

¼ cup water

Coconut Flan with Caramel (Crème Caramel)

Custard

1 cup fresh, canned, or powdered reconstituted coconut milk

1 cup milk

¼ cup sugar

4 eggs

1 tsp vanilla extract

Method

Preheat oven to 375°F. Lightly grease a 8in cake pan and line the bottom with nonstick baking paper.

Combine butter and sugar in a mixing bowl. Cream butter and sugar together until light and fluffy. Add eggs one at a time, beating well after each addition.

Grind bananas in a food processor with the lemon juice.

Process until very mushy. Stir bananas into the mixture.

Add flour, baking soda, cinnamon and coconut, stirring well until fully incorporated

Spoon mixture into prepared cake pan and bake in the preheated oven for 40–45 minutes. Test for doneness by inserting a toothpick into the center of the cake; if it comes out clean, the cake is baked.

Leave cake to cool for 10–15 minutes then turn out onto a cake rack.

Cut into wedges and serve with cream or ice cream.

Ingredients

½ cup butter, at room temperature

1 cup caster sugar

2 eggs

3 bananas

½ cup lemon juice

1½ cups self-rising flour

½ tsp baking soda

½ tsp ground cinnamon

1 cup unsweetened shredded coconut

Banana and Coconut Cake

Tip

If you cannot find self-rising flour, use all-purpose

flour and add 1 tsp baking powder.

Method

To make batter, sift flour in a bowl, and make a well in the center. Combine superfine (caster) sugar, milk, and egg, then mix into flour mixture to make a batter of a smooth consistency. Stand for 10 minutes.

To make sauce, place sugar and water in a saucepan, and cook over a low heat, stirring constantly, until sugar dissolves. Bring to the boil, then reduce heat and simmer, without stirring, for 5 minutes or until mixture is golden.

Remove pan from heat and carefully stir in cream and whisky, if using. Return pan to a low heat and cook, stirring, until combined. Cool.

Beat egg white until soft peaks form, then fold into batter. Heat oil in a saucepan until a cube of bread dropped in browns in 50 seconds. Brush bananas with lime juice, dip in batter to coat then drain off excess. Cook bananas in hot oil for 2–3 minutes or until golden. Serve immediately with sauce.

Banana Fritters

Ingredients

4 large firm bananas, cut in half
then split lengthwise

2 tbsp lime juice

vegetable oil for deep-frying

Batter

1 cup self-rising flour

2 tbsp superfine (caster) sugar

½ cup milk

1 egg, lightly beaten

1 egg white

Caramel sauce

½ cup brown or palm sugar

½ cup water

½ cup cream (double)

2 tsp whisky (optional)

Method

Preheat the oven to 350°F and butter a 9in nonstick cake pan.

Crush the toasted macadamia nuts in a food processor and set aside.

Peel the mangoes and dice the flesh, saving as much juice as possible, then reserve some nice pieces of mango (about ⅓ cup) and process the remaining mango flesh with all the reserved juice. You should have about 1 cup mango purée.

Beat the softened butter and vanilla extract with half the sugar and beat until thick and pale. While beating, add the remaining sugar, and beat until all the sugar has been added. Add the eggs, one at a time, beating well after each addition.

In a separate bowl, mix the crushed nuts, flour, and baking powder together.

Remove the bowl from the mixer and add the flour mixture, stirring well to combine. Add the mango purée and mix gently.

Spoon the batter into the prepared pan, then sprinkle the chopped macadamia nuts and reserved diced mango over the batter and swirl through.

Bake at 340°F for an hour, then remove the cake pan, from the oven and cool in the pan. When cool, remove the cake from the tin. Dredge with powdered sugar.

To prepare the cream, sprinkle the nutmeg over, whip the cream and nutmeg together, until the cream is thick and fragrant. Serve alongside the cake with some mango slices.

Mango Cake with Nutmeg Cream

Ingredients

1 cup unsalted, roasted macadamia nuts

3 large mangos

1 cup butter

1 cup superfine (caster) sugar

1 tsp vanilla extract

4 large eggs

2 cups all-purpose flour

1½ tsp baking powder

½ cup toasted macadamia nuts, chopped

About powdered (icing) sugar

2 cups heavy (double) cream

1 tsp nutmeg

1 mango, sliced, for serving

Method

Mix together all dried ingredients. Add, while stirring, the boiling water, bring to boil, and simmer, still stirring for 10 minutes until thick. Stir in almond extract. Pour into lightly-greased serving bowl, cool, cover, and refrigerate.

Serve with a large bowl of cannedor fresh, peeled lychees, gooseberries, or fresh guava and cream if desired.

Almond Rice Jello

Ingredients

⅓ cup ground rice

⅔ cup ground almonds

4 tbsp powdered unflavored gelatin

⅔ cup superfine (caster) sugar

4 tbsp unsweetened shredded coconut

4½ cups boiling water

few drops of almond extract

Method

Combine the flour and sugar in a mixing bowl. Add the eggs and milk and whisk mixture until smooth.

Heat a skillet. Spray or sprinkle with a little oil, and add enough of the mixture to make a thin pancake. Cook the pancakes for 1–2 minutes each side.

Combine sugar, water, and pandanus leaf in a saucepan. Bring to the boil and simmer over low heat, and stir until sugar dissolves. Add coconut and cook until all the liquid has been absorbed.

Place one tablespoonful of the coconut mixture on each pancake and roll it up like a cigar. Serve pancakes with ice cream.

Coconut Pancakes

Ingredients

½ cup all-purpose flour

1 tbsp superfine sugar

2 eggs, lightly beaten

¾ cup milk or coconut milk

oil spray for cooking

1 cup grated palm sugar or brown sugar

½ cup water

1 pandanus leaf

1 cup unsweetened shredded coconut

Method

Peel the outer layers from the lemongrass stalks, finely chop the lower white bulbous parts, and discard the fibrous tops. Place the lemongrass, sugar, and ½ cup of water in a saucepan. Simmer, stirring, for 5 minutes or until the sugar dissolves, then bring to the boil. Remove from the heat and leave to cool for 20 minutes. Refrigerate for 30 minutes.

Halve the melon and scrape out the seeds. Cut into wedges, then remove the skin and cut the flesh into small chunks. Slice off the two fat sides of the mango close to the stone. Cut a criss-cross pattern across the flesh (but not the skin) of each piece, then push the skin inside out to expose the cubes of flesh and cut them off.

Place the melon, mango and lychees in serving bowls. Strain the lemongrass syrup and pour over the fruit. Decorate with mint.

Oriental Fruit Salad

Ingredients

3 stalks lemongrass

¼ cup superfine (caster) sugar

1 small cantaloupe melon

1 mango

1¾ cups can lychees, drained

fresh mint leaves to garnish

Tip

If you're serving a very spicy or rich meal, give your guests this light and unusual fruit salad to finish.

Index